The
Garden

ISBN 979-8-89130-267-9 (paperback)
ISBN 979-8-89130-268-6 (digital)

Christian Faith Publishing
832 Park Avenue
Meadville, PA 16335
www.christianfaithpublishing.com

Printed in the United States of America

The Garden

Ataya Hilburn

We have a garden in our backyard.

Daddy built the garden for us.

We help Mommy plant seeds in the garden.

Mommy says we have to wait
for the seeds to grow.
Waiting is hard!

We water the seeds every day.

We see the seeds start to sprout!
Our plants are growing!

Our seeds have made a plant!

Our plant has made tomatoes!

We love to eat the food
from our garden!

About the Author

Ataya Hilburn is a wife, mother of two beautiful children, nurse, and follower of Jesus Christ. She has a deep passion for children and letting them be children. It has been her dream since she became a mother to write children's books with simple concepts for families to enjoy together. Her hope is that this book will fill that need for other families.

Printed in the USA
CPSIA information can be obtained
at www.ICGtesting.com
CBHW041944120724
11510CB00035B/1144

9 798891 302679